Contents

Living things need
oxygen to stay alive

Humans can survive without food or water for a short time, but no-one can take a break from breathing. Breathing moves 'fresh' air into, and 'stale' air out of, the body. The air that surrounds us may be invisible, but from the moment of birth it is essential for life.

Gases in the air

Air is not a solid, like iron, or a liquid, like water; it is a gas. It spreads out to fill up any space that it is put into. The air we breathe is a mixture of gases – including nitrogen, oxygen, argon, carbon dioxide and water vapour. Of these gases the most important one, as far as life is concerned, is oxygen.

Oxygen
20.9%

Argon
0.96%

Water vapour
0.1%

Carbon dioxide
0.04%

Nitrogen
78%

What is in air?
Balloon sizes show the percentage of each gas present in the air.

Breathing air
This baby started breathing the moment she was born.

How We
Breathe

Richard Walker

FRANKLIN WATTS

This edition 2007

Franklin Watts
338 Euston Road, London NW1 3BH

Franklin Watts Australia
Level 17/207 Kent Street
Sydney, NSW 2000

Series editor: Adrian Cole
Series design: White Design
Art director: Jonathan Hair
Picture researcher: Diana Morris
Educational consultant: Peter Riley
Medical consultant: Dr Gabrielle Murphy

A CIP catalogue record for this book
is available from the British Library.

ISBN–13: 978 0 7496 7260 7

Printed in Malaysia

Acknowledgements:
W Aldridge/Robert Harding: 25b. Chris Bjornberg/SPL: 18t.
Dr Tony Brain/SPL: 13t. Dr Arnold Brody/SPL: 27c.
Clinique Ste Catherine/CNRI/SPL: 14t. CNRI/SPL: 12b. Colorsport: 21bl.
Corbis: 11t, 20b. Alain Dex, Publiphoto Diffusion/SPL: 24t. Eye of Science/SPL: 11b.
Prof C Ferlaud/CNRI/SPL: 22bc, 22br. Mauro Fermariello/SPL: 27b.
A.Glauberman/SPL: 27tr. Kelly-Mooney Photography/Corbis: 23t.
James King-Holmes/SPL: 19b. Paul Litherland front cover, 28b.
JoeMcBride/Corbis: 16t. Prof P Motta/Dept of Anatomy/
University "La Sapienza", Rome/SPL: 20t.
The Purcell Team/Corbis: 29t. Quest/SPL: 6tr.
Galen Rowell/Corbis: 29b. David Scharf/SPL: 17b.
Dr Gary Settles/SPL: 25t. SPL: 5t.
Tom Stewart Photography/Corbis:4b. Barrie Watts: 9t.

Every attempt has been made to clear copyright.
Should there be any inadvertent omission,
please apply to the publisher for rectification.

Franklin Watts is a division of Hachette Children's Books.

Oxygen supplies

From frogs to foxes, honeybees to humans, living things need to breathe oxygen to stay alive. Plants maintain the levels of oxygen in the environment. In a process called 'photosynthesis', plants make their food using carbon dioxide, water and energy from sunlight. The process also produces oxygen, which flows into the air, so it should never run out.

BOYLE'S PUMP

In the seventeenth century an English scientist called Robert Boyle (1627–91) performed a number of experiments using a vacuum pump. He used the pump to suck out the air from a sealed glass jar containing a mouse. The mouse died. Boyle's experiment seems cruel now but it did prove that air is essential for life.

Boyle's pump

In Boyle's original experiment the air was sucked out of the container and the mouse died.

Breathing assistance

When there is no air around to breathe, for example in thick smoke or poisonous fumes, we cannot simply stop breathing. This is a situation that firefighters have to deal with regularly. They use breathing apparatus to supply them with clean, fresh air so they can avoid suffocating and continue with their work.

Helped to breathe

A firefighter wears breathing apparatus inside a smoke-filled room. He can search for casualties and put out fires without suffocating.

Body cells use
oxygen to release energy

The human body is made up of tiny living units called cells. We breathe in to supply these cells with oxygen. They use the oxygen to release energy from the food that we eat. The process produces carbon dioxide which we breathe out.

It takes about 100 trillion (100,000,000,000,000) cells to make a human being. Every one of these cells needs energy to stay alive.

Brain cells

A micrograph of brain cells. The cells need a constant supply of oxygen to keep them working.

Types of cell

There are over **200** different types of cell in the human body. For example, muscle cells produce body movement. Cells vary in appearance according to what they do, but inside they are all very similar.

Staying alive

The air we breathe and the food we eat are essential for life.

Inside a cell

An outer cell membrane encloses watery, jelly-like cytoplasm. This is where all the chemical reactions take place that keep the cell alive. Floating in the cytoplasm are sausage-shaped mitochondria. These are the cell's power plants. Some cells contain hundreds of mitochondria.

Inside a cell

This section through a 'typical' cell shows its main parts, including the cell's control centre, its nucleus.

BURNING ENERGY

Ask an adult to strike a match, and watch it burn. Using oxygen in the air, energy stored in the match is turned into heat energy you can feel, and light energy you can see. Something similar happens inside mitochondria, but under more controlled conditions. Glucose is 'burned' to release chemical energy that keeps cells working and a small amount of heat energy that keeps you warm.

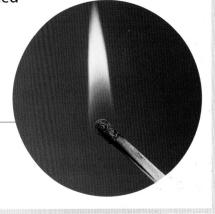

Burning match

This releases all its energy rapidly as heat and light. The release of energy from a cell is more controlled.

Cytoplasm
the clear jelly-like substance between the nucleus and the cell membrane

Mitochondrion
provides the energy for the cell's activities

Cell membrane
the protective covering

Nucleus
contains the information that directs the cell's activities

Mitochondrion

This cut-away shows the folded inner membrane where cell respiration takes place. The mitochondrion releases energy constantly.

Energy
keeps the cell alive

Releasing energy

Energy is released inside mitochondria by a process called cell respiration. Cell respiration uses oxygen to release energy from food, such as glucose, to fuel the cell's chemical reactions and keep it alive. Cell respiration also produces a waste product, carbon dioxide. This gas would poison the body if allowed to build up, so it is carried by blood to the lungs and breathed out.

Glucose
from the food we eat

Oxygen
from the air we breathe

Carbon dioxide
carried to the lungs and breathed out

The respiratory system takes
oxygen into the body

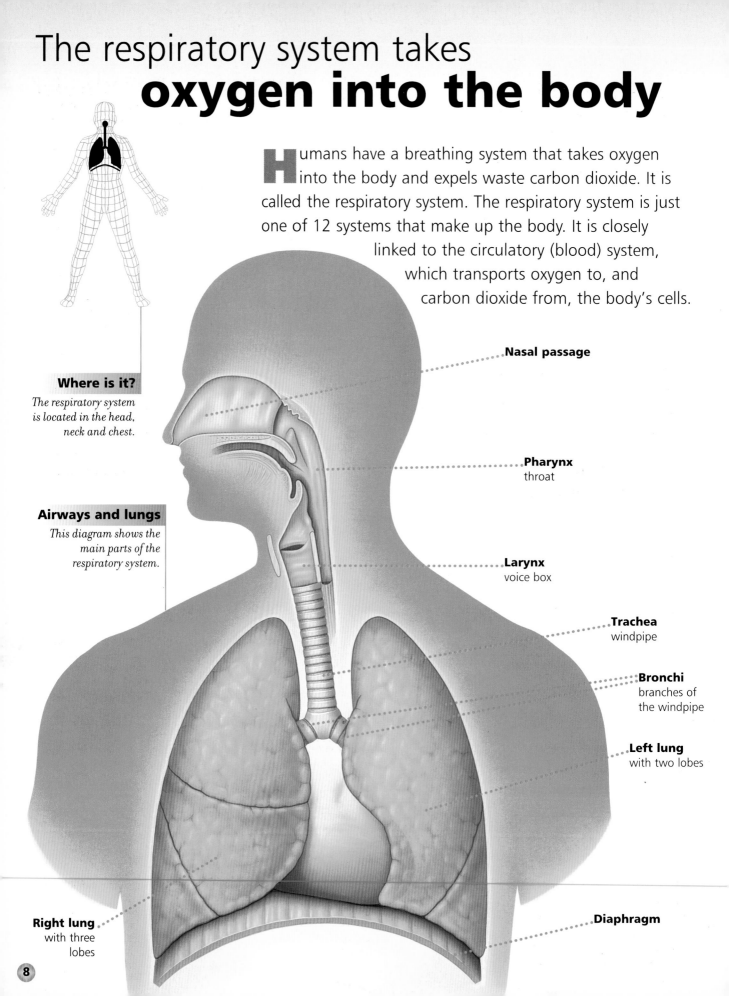

Humans have a breathing system that takes oxygen into the body and expels waste carbon dioxide. It is called the respiratory system. The respiratory system is just one of 12 systems that make up the body. It is closely linked to the circulatory (blood) system, which transports oxygen to, and carbon dioxide from, the body's cells.

Where is it?

The respiratory system is located in the head, neck and chest.

Airways and lungs

This diagram shows the main parts of the respiratory system.

Nasal passage

Pharynx
throat

Larynx
voice box

Trachea
windpipe

Bronchi
branches of the windpipe

Left lung
with two lobes

Right lung
with three lobes

Diaphragm

OTHER ANIMALS

Mammals and birds also take in oxygen and get rid of carbon dioxide through their lungs. Other animals do things differently. Amphibians, such as this frog, have lungs but also absorb oxygen through their moist skin.

Breathing skin

A frog breathes through its moist skin when it hibernates for the winter.

Respiratory system

The respiratory system consists of air passages – the nose, throat, trachea and bronchi – that carry air, and the tissue that forms the two lungs. The lungs have a moist inner lining through which oxygen passes into the blood and is exchanged for carbon dioxide (see pages 16–17).

Circulatory system

Blood picks up oxygen in the lungs and carries it the short distance to the heart, which then pumps it to every cell in the body. These cells then dump waste carbon dioxide into the blood, which carries it back to the lungs to be breathed out (see pages 16–17).

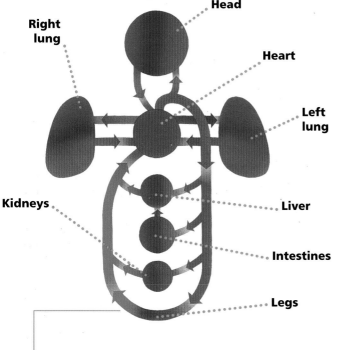

Head

Right lung

Heart

Left lung

Kidneys

Liver

Intestines

Legs

Circulatory system

A diagramatic representation of the blood circulatory system. The heart pumps blood rich in oxygen (shown in red) to the cells, and blood poor in oxygen (shown in blue) back to the heart and into the lungs where the carbon dioxide is exchanged for more oxygen.

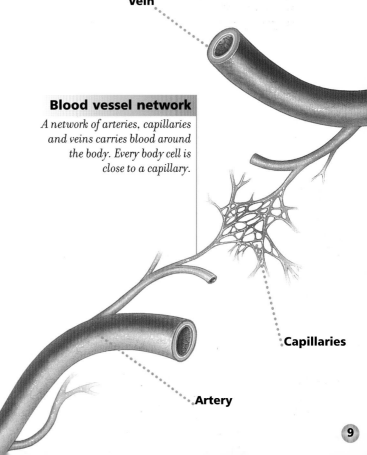

Vein

Blood vessel network

A network of arteries, capillaries and veins carries blood around the body. Every body cell is close to a capillary.

Capillaries

Artery

Breathed-in air is
warmed and cleaned

The nose and throat form the first section of the respiratory system. The nose warms, cleans and moistens the air breathed in because the lungs would be damaged if the air was cold, dirty or dry. Of course, air can also be breathed in through the mouth, but the nose removes most of the bacteria and other germs from the air, before it passes into the throat on its way to the lungs. That is why it is better, if possible, to breathe in through the nose.

Inside the nose

The nose has two nostrils. These are the entrances to the nasal cavity. Breathed-in (inhaled) air passes through here and becomes wetter as it picks up moisture from the lining of the nasal cavity. The air also gets warmer because there are lots of blood vessels in the nasal cavity that give off heat, like tiny radiators.

Nasal cavity
lined with cilia and mucus-secreting glands – inhaled air becomes warm, moist and clean (see opposite)

Nostrils
entrance to the nasal cavity

Pharynx
throat

Mouth
air can be breathed in through here, too

Larynx
voice box

Epiglottis
closes the windpipe off from the throat when food is being swallowed

Nose and throat
A section through the head showing the nasal cavity and the throat.

CATCHING A COLD

The nose does not always manage to filter out viruses. Viruses can infect the respiratory system and cause a 'cold'. This viral infection is picked-up from contact with, or breathing in water vapour from, other infected people. Once inside the body, viruses irritate the throat and the nasal cavity. This produces a lot more mucus than normal, causing you to have a stuffy, runny nose.

Runny nose

Blowing your nose into a handkerchief gets rid of extra mucus when you have a cold and helps to stop the virus spreading.

Nostril hair

If you look up the nostrils of someone's nose you will see that they are quite hairy. As air is inhaled through these hairs, they act like a net which traps larger bits of dust and dirt.

Mucus and cilia

Dust, dirt or bacteria that pass the nostril hairs gets stuck in a thick, sticky liquid called mucus. A thin layer of mucus covers the lining of the nasal cavity. Underneath the mucus are millions of tiny hair-like cilia. They bend to and fro, sweeping the dirty mucus towards the throat. Here it is swallowed and digested in the stomach, which kills any bacteria.

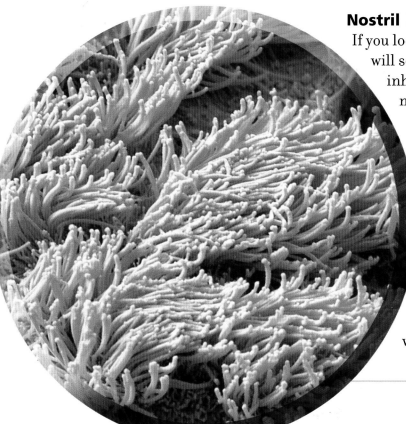

Inside the nose

This micrograph shows the tiny hair-like cilia inside the nose that beat rhythmically to remove dirt. Cilia cannot be seen with the human eye.

The network of
passages carries air

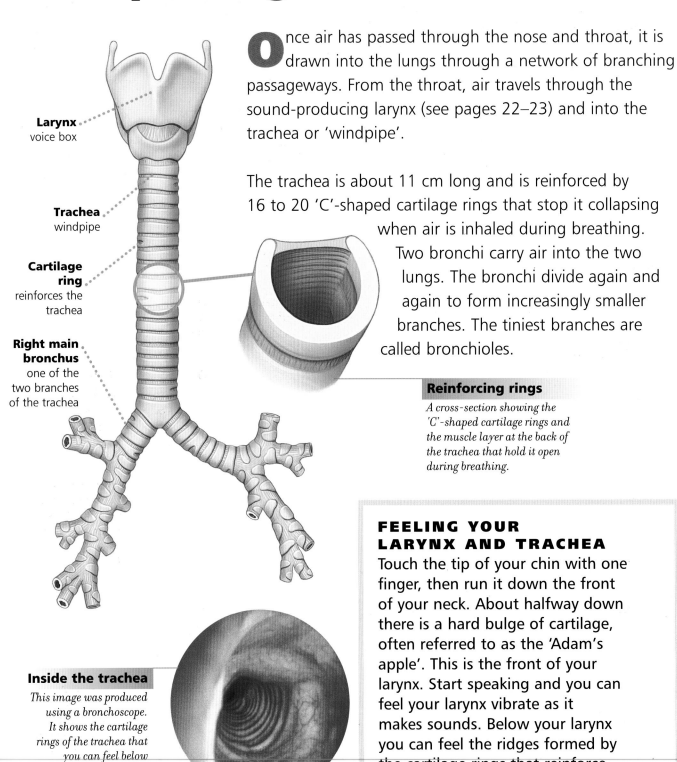

O nce air has passed through the nose and throat, it is drawn into the lungs through a network of branching passageways. From the throat, air travels through the sound-producing larynx (see pages 22–23) and into the trachea or 'windpipe'.

The trachea is about 11 cm long and is reinforced by 16 to 20 'C'-shaped cartilage rings that stop it collapsing when air is inhaled during breathing. Two bronchi carry air into the two lungs. The bronchi divide again and again to form increasingly smaller branches. The tiniest branches are called bronchioles.

Larynx
voice box

Trachea
windpipe

Cartilage ring
reinforces the trachea

Right main bronchus
one of the two branches of the trachea

Reinforcing rings

A cross-section showing the 'C'-shaped cartilage rings and the muscle layer at the back of the trachea that hold it open during breathing.

Inside the trachea

This image was produced using a bronchoscope. It shows the cartilage rings of the trachea that you can feel below your larynx.

FEELING YOUR LARYNX AND TRACHEA

Touch the tip of your chin with one finger, then run it down the front of your neck. About halfway down there is a hard bulge of cartilage, often referred to as the 'Adam's apple'. This is the front of your larynx. Start speaking and you can feel your larynx vibrate as it makes sounds. Below your larynx you can feel the ridges formed by the cartilage rings that reinforce your trachea.

Clean sweep

The air-cleaning process continues in the trachea and bronchi where more sticky mucus traps dirt, dust and bacteria. Cilia, like those found in the nose, waft the dirty mucus upwards to the throat where it is swallowed and destroyed.

Carpet of cilia

The cilia in the trachea work constantly to clear dirt-laden mucus.

Bronchial tree

The passageways that carry air between the throat and lungs are sometimes called the 'bronchial tree' because they look like an upside-down tree. The tree's 'trunk' is the trachea, its 'branches' are the bronchi, while bronchioles form its 'twigs'.

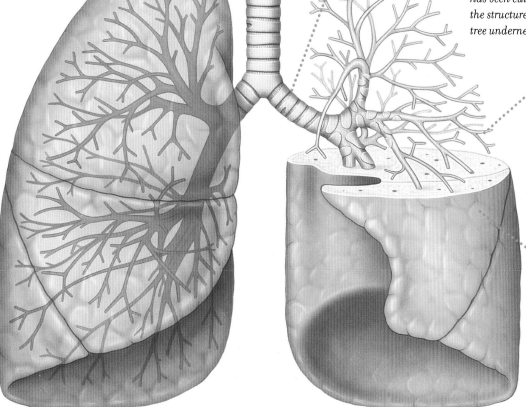

Trachea
this forms the 'trunk' of the tree

Left main bronchus
one of the two tubes that form the 'branches' of the tree

The bronchial tree
The top surface of the left lung has been cut away to reveal the structure of the bronchial tree underneath.

Lobe of right lung
the bronchioles are not normally visible through the lung

Bronchioles
there are around 30,000 of these in the lung, which form the 'twigs' of the tree

Lobe of left lung
the top of the lung has been cut away to reveal the structure of the bronchioles

The structure of
the lungs

The lungs are light and spongy because they are filled with branching air-filled passages – the bronchi and bronchioles – that end in tiny air bags. The lungs fill most of the space inside the chest. They 'sit' on the diaphragm, the dome-shaped sheet of muscle used in breathing (see pages 18–19). They are surrounded by the rib cage, which protects them from damage.

Filling the chest

This CT scan shows a 'slice' through the chest, seen from below. It reveals that the two lungs almost fill up the entire chest.

Rib cage

Right lung

Left lung

Heart

Spinal column
(backbone) supports the body

Right main bronchus
one of the two air passages into the lungs

Trachea
carries air into the chest

Right lung
(shown cut away) is larger than the left lung

Heart
pumps blood

Rib cage
surrounds and protects the lungs

Diaphragm
a sheet of muscle that plays an important part in breathing

Left lung
is smaller than the right lung because it shares space with the heart

Inside the chest

A view inside the chest showing the position of the lungs and heart. The ribs have been cut away and the right lung cut open. The lungs are pink in colour because of their rich blood supply.

Blood supply

The lungs have their own blood supply from the heart. Blood low in oxygen is pumped by the heart to the lungs along the pulmonary arteries. These branch and carry blood to all parts of the lungs. The smallest blood vessels – capillaries – join together to form the pulmonary veins which carry blood rich in oxygen back to the heart.

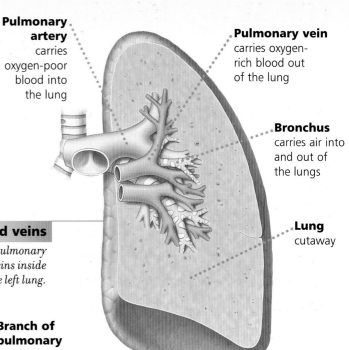

Pulmonary artery
carries oxygen-poor blood into the lung

Pulmonary vein
carries oxygen-rich blood out of the lung

Bronchus
carries air into and out of the lungs

Lung
cutaway

Arteries and veins
The branching pulmonary artery and veins inside the left lung.

Branch of pulmonary vein

Branch of pulmonary artery

Alveolus
cutaway

Alveoli and capillaries
A bunch of alveoli surrounded by a web of capillaries through which oxygen and carbon dioxide are exchanged.

MODEL OF ALVEOLI

Make a model of the interior of the lungs. Take a string bag – the sort supermarkets pack oranges in – and fill it with ping pong balls. The balls represent alveoli and the string the blood capillaries around them.

Air bags

At the end of the narrowest bronchioles there are microscopic air sacs called alveoli (one air sac is called an alveolus). They look like bunches of grapes. Altogether there are about 300 million alveoli in both lungs.

Oxygen enters the blood and is
carried to the body cells

Oxygen gets into the blood through the millions of sac-like alveoli in the lungs. The alveoli provide an enormous surface area packed into a small space inside the chest. Each second we receive the oxygen the body needs, and rapidly get rid of poisonous carbon dioxide that it does not.

Gas exchange process

A section through an alveolus and blood capillary showing the exchange of gases in the lungs.

Capillary
carries carbon dioxide-rich blood from the rest of the body, via the heart, to the lungs to be expelled

Alveolus

Carbon dioxide

Oxygen

Carbon dioxide leaving the blood

Oxygen entering the blood

Capillary
carries oxygen-rich blood to the rest of the body via the heart

Massive surface

If they could be spread out, our alveoli would cover an area three-quarters the size of a tennis court.

Exchanging gases

When we breathe in, oxygen from the air dissolves in the thin layer of moisture lining an alveolus. It then passes through the wall of the alveolus, and that of the capillary surrounding it, into the blood. That distance is tiny – just 0.0005 mm. Waste carbon dioxide moves in the opposite direction from the blood to the alveolus and is breathed out.

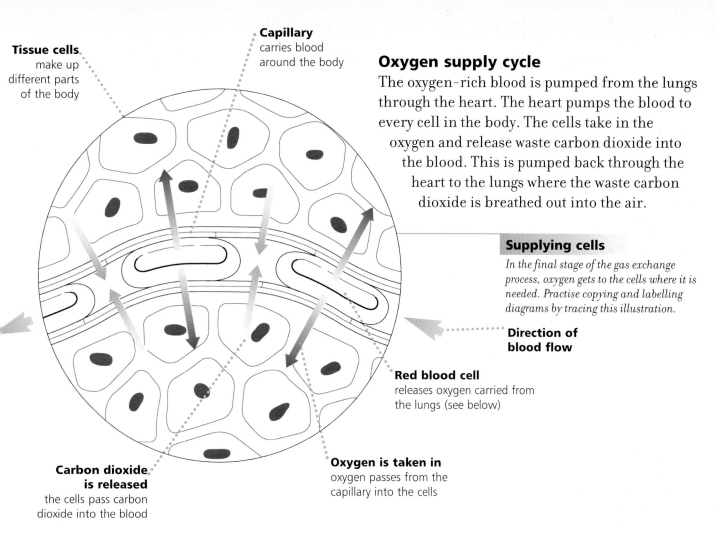

Tissue cells
make up
different parts
of the body

Capillary
carries blood
around the body

Oxygen supply cycle

The oxygen-rich blood is pumped from the lungs through the heart. The heart pumps the blood to every cell in the body. The cells take in the oxygen and release waste carbon dioxide into the blood. This is pumped back through the heart to the lungs where the waste carbon dioxide is breathed out into the air.

Supplying cells

In the final stage of the gas exchange process, oxygen gets to the cells where it is needed. Practise copying and labelling diagrams by tracing this illustration.

Direction of blood flow

Red blood cell
releases oxygen carried from the lungs (see below)

Oxygen is taken in
oxygen passes from the capillary into the cells

Carbon dioxide is released
the cells pass carbon dioxide into the blood

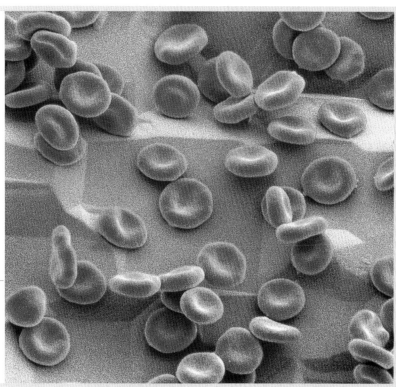

OXYGEN CARRIERS

A single drop of blood contains over 250 million red blood cells like these. Each cell is packed with a substance called 'haemoglobin'. This has the ability to pick up oxygen where there is plenty of it – in the lungs – and release oxygen where it is in short supply – in the tissues.

Red blood cells

The rounded, doughnut shape is ideal for quickly picking up, or releasing, lots of oxygen.

Muscles move air
into and out of the lungs

Breathing sucks fresh air into the lungs and pushes stale air out, bringing in oxygen and removing carbon dioxide. However, the lungs have no muscles and cannot expand or contract on their own. To breathe, the respiratory muscles (the diaphragm and the muscles connecting the ribs) alter the size of the chest. This moves air in and out of the lungs.

Inhaling

To breathe in, or inhale, the diaphragm contracts and flattens. The intercostal muscles – the ones between the ribs – contract to pull the ribs upwards and outwards. Together these actions make a larger volume (space) inside the chest and lungs. This extra space is filled by the air that is sucked into the lungs from outside.

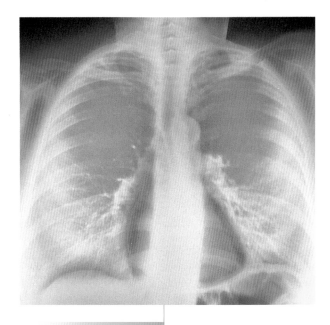

Lung movers

This X-ray shows the lungs (coloured light purple on the left and right) inside the chest surrounded by the ribs.

Air in

The diaphragm pushes down, and the ribs are pulled up, filling the lungs with air.

Exhaling

To breathe out, or exhale, the diaphragm relaxes and becomes dome-shaped again. The intercostal muscles relax and the ribs move downwards and inwards. The space inside the chest decreases, the lungs are squeezed and air is forced out through the nose or mouth.

Diaphragm

Air out

The diaphragm relaxes, the ribs move down and air is forced out of the lungs.

EXPANDING CHEST

Put a tape measure around the ribs of a friend's chest. Ask them to breathe out, and then take a measurement. Ask them to breathe in, and take another measurement. Draw a bar chart with two bars – one for breathing in and one for breathing out – to compare chest sizes. You should find the chest gets bigger when breathing in.

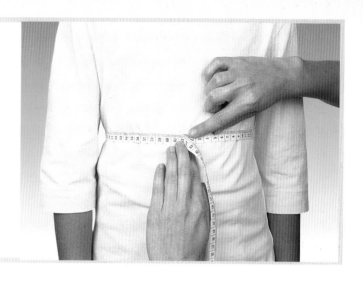

Gas	% in inhaled air
Oxygen	20.9
Carbon dioxide	0.04
Water vapour	0.1
Argon	0.96
Nitrogen	78

Gas	% in exhaled air
Oxygen	16
Carbon dioxide	4.0
Water vapour	1.04
Argon	0.96
Nitrogen	78

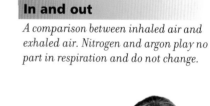

% in inhaled air   **% in exhaled air**

In and out

A comparison between inhaled air and exhaled air. Nitrogen and argon play no part in respiration and do not change.

More or less?

Gas exchange (see pages 16–17) removes oxygen from air in the lungs and adds carbon dioxide, so exhaled air contains less oxygen and more carbon dioxide than inhaled air. Exhaled air also has more water vapour, picked up from the moist lining of the lungs.

Spirometer

This man is breathing into a spirometer to measure the volume of air passing into or out of his lungs.

19

The breathing rate changes
during exercise

During exercise we breathe faster and the heart beats more quickly. This supplies the body with the extra oxygen it needs and removes more waste carbon dioxide.

At rest, for example when reading a book, we probably breathe in and out between 12 to 15 times a minute. But during exercise the breathing rate can double, up to 30 times a minute.

Demanding muscles

Every body movement is caused by the contraction of muscles. They use energy to contract, or get shorter. To release the energy, muscle cells, like other body cells, need oxygen. Muscle cells need more energy and more oxygen during longer periods of activity.

Oxygen supply

This snaking blood capillary (blue) carries oxygen to muscle cells (red).

On the move

These cyclists are breathing faster than they would if they were resting because their muscle cells need more oxygen to release more energy.

Breathing control

We do not have to think about breathing faster when taking exercise. The brain does it automatically. As the body becomes more active, the brain stem at the base of the brain sends a message to the diaphragm and intercostal muscles. It tells them to contract faster, which increases the breathing rate.

Breathing rate

The brain stem increases or decreases the breathing rate according to whether you are active or resting.

Brain stem
tells the diaphragm and intercostal muscles to contract faster

Recovery time

Athlete Cathy Freeman gulps in extra air to get more oxygen to her cells after completing a 400-metre race.

Outgoing message
the brain sends messages to the respiratory muscles

Incoming message
tells the brain that the body is more active

Out of breath

During short bursts of intense exercise, such as sprinting, muscles run out of oxygen. For a short time they can release energy for movement without oxygen. But this builds up wastes that need extra oxygen to remove them when we rest. That is why we 'pant' after sprinting.

HOW FAST?

You will need a watch or clock for this activity. Sit quietly and count how many breaths (in and out counts as one) you make in one minute. Now run on the spot for 2 minutes, then immediately count your breaths again. Plot your results on a bar chart to make a clear comparison between the different rates.

The larynx, tongue and lips
produce sounds

Of all the animals on Earth, humans are the only ones that can communicate with each other using spoken language. We produce sounds in the larynx, or 'voice box'. These basic sounds are then turned into words that we and other people understand. The whole process is controlled by the brain.

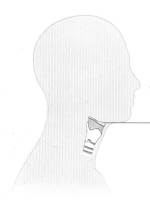

Epiglottis
closes the windpipe off from the throat when food is being swallowed

Larynx link

The larynx links the pharynx (throat) and trachea.

Vocal cords
folds of tissue open and close to produce different sounds

Adam's apple
a piece of cartilage that protects the vocal cords

Voice box

The larynx is made up of pieces of cartilage. It provides an open passageway to allow air in and out of the trachea. Stretched across it from front to back are the two vocal cords.

Rings of cartilage
reinforce the trachea

Trachea
windpipe that leads to the lungs

Vocal cords

Vocal cords are two folds of tissue that can be opened or closed across the larynx. During normal breathing they are open. To produce sounds, they are pulled closer together. When we breathe out, air is forced between the vocal cords, causing them to vibrate and make sounds.

Open and closed

This view into the larynx shows the vocal cords open and closed (far right). The epiglottis is the white area above the vocal cords.

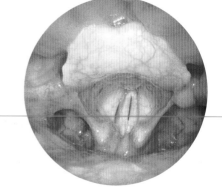

Pitch and volume

Tight, thin vocal cords vibrate faster and produce higher-pitched sounds than thick vocal cords. Men have thick vocal cords that vibrate slowly, which is why they have lower-pitched voices than women. The faster the air passes between the vocal cords, the louder the volume of the sound.

Speech producers

To produce speech, sound waves – vibrations in the air – pass from the larynx up the throat, and through the mouth and nasal cavity. The sounds become louder and clearer. The tongue and lips move and turn basic sounds into the vowels (such as 'a' and 'e') and consonants (such as 'l' and 't') that together make up spoken language.

Sound control

People who act, sing, or play wind instruments such as a trumpet, need to develop good breathing control. For example, to keep in tune with music, singers have to produce sounds of the right pitch and volume. They do this by changing the shape and tension of their vocals cords, and by adjusting the speed of the air that passes through them.

TONGUE-TIED

Your tongue plays a key role in producing speech. Conduct this experiment to see how well you can speak without it. Press the tip of your tongue behind your upper front teeth. Now try to recite the alphabet. Without your tongue the letters are barely recognisable!

Coughing, sneezing and other
breathing movements

As well as regular breathing and making speech, the respiratory system can produce other movements, such as coughing, sneezing, hiccuping and laughing. Some of these movements, such as coughing, help to protect the respiratory system. Other breathing movements, such as laughing, help to show emotion.

Coughing and sneezing

Coughing helps to protect the respiratory system by clearing out any irritating dust or mucus. First, we take a deep breath. Then the vocal cords shut to trap air inside the lungs. This makes air pressure build up inside the lungs. Then, suddenly, the vocal cords fly open. Air rushes out from the lungs, clearing any irritations away, and escapes from the mouth at up to **160 kph**. Sneezing works in the same way, but the air blast comes out mainly through the nose.

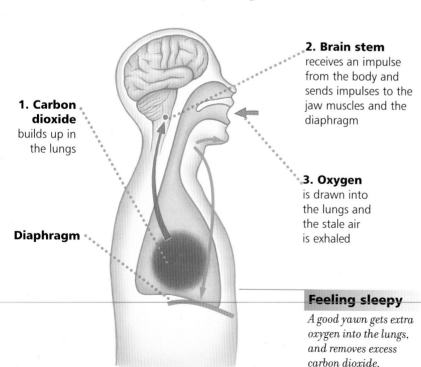

1. Carbon dioxide builds up in the lungs

2. Brain stem receives an impulse from the body and sends impulses to the jaw muscles and the diaphragm

3. Oxygen is drawn into the lungs and the stale air is exhaled

Diaphragm

Feeling sleepy
A good yawn gets extra oxygen into the lungs, and removes excess carbon dioxide.

Coughing
Coughing is an important safety feature of the respiratory system. This woman is coughing to clear an irritation in her throat. Coughing can also help clear blockages in more serious cases, such as when someone is choking on a piece of food. Always cover your mouth when you cough as this will help to prevent the spread of germs.

Yawning

Yawning seems to occur as a result of an increase in levels of carbon dioxide in the blood – for example if the breathing rate slows down. To 'flush out' the stale air from the lungs, the brain sends impulses to muscles in the body. These force the mouth open and make us inhale deeply, and then breathe out.

PHOTOGRAPHING A SNEEZE

By using a special technique called 'schlieren photography' it is possible to photograph a sneeze. The camera detects turbulence in the air and photographs the high speed gust of air and mucus droplets produced by a sneezing person.

Man sneezing

This schlieren photograph shows what happens when a person sneezes. It's easy to see how germs spread when someone with a cold sneezes!

Hiccuping

Hiccuping occurs when the diaphragm is irritated. Instead of flattening smoothly, it contracts in jerky spasms. This sucks air into the lungs in short bursts, making the vocal cords snap shut to produce that familiar 'hiccup' sound.

Laughing

We laugh when we are feeling happy and amused. In order to laugh, we take a deep breath in, and then breathe out the air in a number of short bursts accompanied by 'laughing' sounds.

Feeling good

Laughing makes the body release chemicals called endorphins that make you feel relaxed.

Problems that make it
hard to breathe

There are many factors that have an effect on breathing and health. They include asthma and cigarette smoking. Although they are very two different things, they both affect what happens when some people breathe.

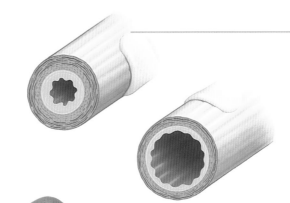

Narrowed tubes

Here you can see the difference between a normal bronchiole and one narrowed during an asthma attack.

Asthma

Asthma is a respiratory disorder that affects about **1** in every **8** children (and **1** in every **13** adults). During an asthma attack, tiny muscles in the outer layer of the bronchioles in the lungs pull tighter and make the tubes narrower. The lining of these bronchioles also becomes inflamed and swollen. This slows the flow of air in and out of the lungs, resulting in shortness of breath, wheezing, coughing and, in serious attacks, death. People who suffer from asthma attacks get relief by using special inhalers. These squirt a drug into inhaled air that makes the bronchioles relax and return to their normal width.

Possible causes

Asthma has a number of causes. It can be triggered by breathing in pollen grains from plants, the droppings of dust mites, skin flakes or hair from animals. But other causes can include sudden exercise, cold air, infections or pollution from cars or factories.

Using an inhaler

Most asthma sufferers lead a normal life. They use special inhalers to prevent them having an attack. However, in serious cases, some sufferers may still have an attack that requires medical attention.

Smoking

Cigarette smoking is a major cause of human illness. The smoke that is breathed in contains a number of irritants and poisons. Tar irritates and inflames the tissue of the lungs and can cause lung cancer, a disease which can kill. Carbon monoxide poisons the blood and stops it from carrying oxygen properly.

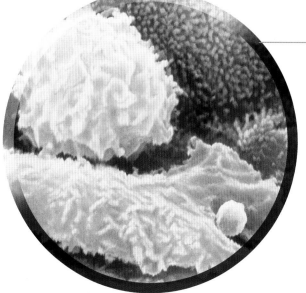

Dust busters

This micrograph shows a normal alveolar macrophage (top) and one that has changed shape to engulf the dust particle (in green).

Comparing lungs

Notice the difference between a pink healthy lung (left) and a black, damaged smoker's lung.

Lung cleaners

Dust cells, called alveolar macrophages, roam around lung tissue looking for any dust particles that might cause damage. They engulf any particles and are then swept up to the throat and swallowed. The poisons in cigarette smoke encourage lung damage by preventing alveolar macrophages working normally.

ARTIFICIAL RESPIRATION

If a person stops breathing even for just a few minutes, their brain will be deprived of vital oxygen and will be damaged. Artificial respiration is therefore an important part of first aid, but should only be done by someone who is trained. In artificial respiration the helper breathes into the patient's mouth to inflate the lungs so that they start working again.

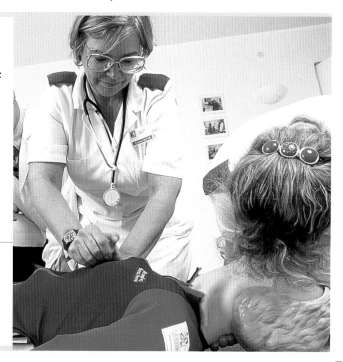

Saving a life

These nurses are using a dummy to practise life-saving CPR, used when a patient has stopped breathing and their heart is not beating. It includes breathing into the patient's mouth.

Surviving in places
where oxygen is scarce

People need oxygen to live, but we can still survive in places where oxygen is scarce. There is less oxygen the further we go up into the Earth's atmosphere. In the oceans there is oxygen in the water, but we cannot use it. Yet people can dive, fly and climb.

Underwater

Unlike the gills of fish, human lungs cannot take in oxygen from water. Instead divers use an invention called 'scuba' (Self-Contained Underwater Breathing Apparatus) equipment. Air from tanks enters the lungs at around the same pressure as the surrounding water, enabling the diver to breathe underwater.

THE BENDS

As these divers descend, the water pressure increases. This makes nitrogen, a gas found in the air we breathe, dissolve in their blood. If they return to the surface quickly, the nitrogen forms bubbles in their blood, like those in a fizzy pop bottle when the top is unscrewed. This condition is called 'the bends'. It can cause unconsciousness and pain in body joints. Once on the surface, divers suffering from the bends have to rest inside a 'decompression' chamber until they are well again.

Deep dives

Scuba equipment allows divers to breathe underwater for long periods.

High fliers

Modern passenger jet aeroplanes fly at over 10,000 metres, above the highest mountains. At this height oxygen is scarce. For people to breathe, the air inside the aeroplane cabin is kept under pressure, at the same level as air found at lower altitudes. This ensures there is enough oxygen for everyone to breathe. If there is an emergency and the aeroplane depressurises, masks drop from the ceiling. The masks are connected to an oxygen supply, and people use them to breathe. Otherwise they would pass out.

Under pressure

Air is kept under pressure in aeroplane cabins, such as this one, so that people can breathe normally.

High altitude

The higher people go in the atmosphere, the lower the air pressure and the less oxygen there is to breathe. People who live at high altitudes have adapted to lower oxygen levels. They breathe slightly faster than people who normally live at sea level. Their blood contains more red blood cells to carry extra oxygen to their body cells.

Mountain people

These people from the Andes mountain range in South America survive despite lower levels of oxygen in the air. People from low altitudes who climb mountains know that they have to acclimatise to the height. If the climber ascends too quickly, he or she can suffer from headaches, dizziness and breathlessness typical of altitude sickness.

Glossary

Abdomen Part of the body between the chest and the pelvis.

Alveoli (singular: Alveolus) Tiny air bags inside lungs through which oxygen enters the blood.

Amphibians Four-legged, moist-skinned animals, including frogs, that live on land and in water.

Bacteria Group of living things that consist of one simple cell, some of which cause disease.

Blood vessel Tube, such as an artery, vein, or capillary, that carries blood through the body.

Brain Part of the nervous system in the head that controls the body's activities and enables it to feel and think.

Bronchi (singular: Bronchus) Air passages that carry air into and throughout the lungs.

Bronchiole Smallest air passage in the lungs that carries air from bronchi to alveoli.

Capillary Tiny blood vessel that carries blood to and from the body's cells.

Carbon dioxide Gas that is the waste product of cell respiration.

Cartilage Tough, flexible material that forms part of larynx, and supports the ears and nose.

Cell One of trillions of tiny living units that make up the human body.

Cell respiration Process that occurs in cells, using glucose and oxygen to release energy.

Cilia Tiny hair-like structures that beat to move mucus and dirt out of the respiratory system.

Circulatory (blood) system Body system that carries oxygen, and other substances, in the blood to all body cells and removes the waste.

Contract To get shorter, as a muscle does, in order to move part of the body.

CPR (cardiopulmonary respiration) Life-saving technique used when a person stops breathing and their heart stops beating.

CT (computed tomography) scan Special type of X-ray that uses computers to form images of the inside of the living body.

Energy The capacity to do work.

Exhaling Breathing out.

Gas Substance, such as oxygen in the air, that has no definite shape or volume.

Germs General term for microscopic living things (micro-organisms), such as bacteria and viruses, that may cause disease.

Glucose Sugar obtained from food that is the body's main source of energy.

Haemoglobin Red substance found inside red blood cells that carries oxygen.

Inhaling Breathing in.

Larynx (voice box) is the part of the respiratory system that produces sounds.

Mitochondria Sausage-shaped components of cells that carry out cell respiration.

Mucus Thick, slippery liquid produced by the lining of the respiratory system.

Muscles Body tissues that use energy to contract (get shorter) and relax and so move parts of the body.

Oxygen Gas found in the air that is essential for releasing the energy needed for life during cell respiration.

Photosynthesis Process by which plants make food using carbon dioxide, water and sunlight, releasing oxygen as a waste product.

Pollen Tiny particles released by plants into the air as part of plant reproduction.

Pressure The force that presses down on a certain area or surface.

Red blood cells Doughnut-shaped cells found in the blood that carry oxygen from the lungs to the tissues.

Respiratory system Body system that takes oxygen into the body and removes waste carbon dioxide.

Trachea (windpipe) is the tube that carries air to and from the lungs between the larynx and bronchi.

Virus(es) Group of living particles that cause disease in humans and other living things.

Volume The amount of space inside, or occupied by, something.

Water vapour Water in the form of a gas, as it is usually found in the air.

Find out more

These are just some of the websites where you can find out more information about how we breathe. Many of the websites also provide information and illustrations about other systems and processes of the human body.

Note to parents and teachers
Every effort has been made by the Publishers to ensure that these websites are suitable for children; that they are of the highest educational value, and that they contain no inappropriate or offensive material. However, because of the nature of the Internet, it is impossible to guarantee that the contents of these sites will not be altered. We strongly advise that Internet access is supervised by a responsible adult.

www.bbc.co.uk/health/kids/breathing.shtml
Information about breathing and respiratory health.

www.brainpop.com/health/respiratorysystem
Quizzes, movies and lots more information about breathing, speech, asthma, and smoking.

http://yucky.kids.discovery.com/flash/body
Lots to find out about breathing and all other aspects of 'your gross and cool body'.

www.asthma.org.uk
Find out all about asthma at this website from Asthma UK. There is also a test to see if you can identify the parts of the respiratory system and an asthma-related games arcade.

www.ash.org.uk/html/passive/html/kidsbrief.html
Information about the effects of passive smoking and how it affects breathing from Action on Smoking and Health (ASH).

www.planet-science.com
Detailed science website including information about breathing, air pollution, and more.

www.kidshealth.org
Contains information about lungs and keeping them healthy, as well as sneezing and hiccups.

http://faculty.washington.edu/chudler/yawning.html
Everything you need to know about yawning including what makes you yawn.

www.innerbody.com/htm/body.html
Explore different parts of the human body, including the respiratory system.

www.sciencemuseum.org.uk/wellcome-wing/antenna/index.asp
Find out about the latest science and technology exhibitions and news. This site is regularly updated and often features articles on current health issues.

www.lungnet.org.au
The Australian Lung Foundation's Guide to lung health. Click on 'learn about lung health' to find out more information about how the lungs work.

Index